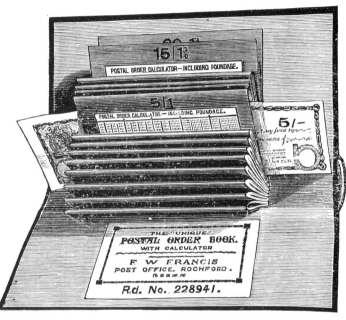

Bygone
ROCHFORD

St Andrew's church.

Bygone
ROCHFORD

L.E.Jerram-Burrows

Phillimore

1988

Published by
PHILLIMORE & CO. LTD.
Shopwyke Hall, Chichester, Sussex

ISBN 0 85033 661 9

Printed and bound in Great Britain by
BIDDLES LTD.
Guildford, Surrey

This book is dedicated to my beloved daughter,
Peta Margaret Pinder,
her husband, Bruce,
and their children, Donna, Nicola and Damian.

List of Illustrations

Frontispiece: St Andrew's church.

BLINKHORNS Chartered Accountants

Client	
Subject	

File No.	Ref.
Prepared by	Date / /
Reviewed by	Date / /
Accounting Dates from / /	to / /

Whispering post / Kings Hill

Last replaced ?1935 by ~~Frank~~ Cyril Smoothy

Preface and Acknowledgements

Following the death of Mrs. J. K. Payne who had originally been asked by the publishers to write this book, I was myself commissioned to undertake the work and this I have greatly enjoyed doing, especially as Jessie Payne and her family were life-long friends of mine. However, the assignment could not have been achieved in so short a time without the help of those of my friends who realised the importance of this golden opportunity to get into print for all time many of the old pictures which for years have been circulating the area.

To all those who have so kindly provided me with illustrations or have helped and encouraged me in any way I tender my sincere thanks, more particularly to Mr. Victor Gray, the County Archivist, and his staff at the Essex Record Office both at Chelmsford and Southend, and for permission to use photograph no. 102; from the Payne Collection nos. 6, 7, 10, 11, 15, 28, 32, 37, 38, 39, 45, 46, 47, 54, 62, 63, 67, 69, 73, 87, 96, 107, 113, 131, 135; to the Committee of the Rochford Amenities Society and particularly to Miss Beryl Webb, their Chairman, who have so kindly allowed me to draw on their collection of pictures and those of the late S. C. Harris deposited in the Essex Record Office, nos. 55, 65, 142, 143; to Peter and Betty Whittingham for their unfailing and tireless help throughout, as well as for reading through the manuscript, and for lending me illustrations nos. 22, 41, 56, 59, 81, 95, 97, 119, 125; to Arthur Stephenson for lending me illustrations nos. 14, 17, 19, 26, 30, 33, 42, 64, 71, 88, 92, 93, 94, 99, 111, 112, 123, 130, 136; to Thora Morley for nos. 5, 34, 35, 53, 57, 75, 79, 80, 129, 139, 141, 149; Lynn Tait Gallery for nos. 27, 43, 61, 70, 77, 78, 88, 90, 91, 110, 118, 138; David Collins for nos. 86, 100, 144, 146; G. F. Sims for nos. 152, 153, 154, 155; John Willson for nos. 114, 115; to Margaret Goddard for no. 52; and to Norman Barnes, the Southend artist, for his willingness to provide me with excellent sketches, reproduced as nos. 2, 9, 13, 103, 156. I would also like to thank Mr. Charles Bruce for the frontispiece and nos. 137 and 148.

Rochford, encircled as it is by a group of interesting and mainly marshland villages, has long since been acknowledged as one of the most historic townships in Essex. Only a tiny part of Rochford's story can be included in this book, for its roots go back over a thousand years with more history than can be crammed into one volume. If, as you turn these pages, you become fired with enthusiasm and have a burning desire to learn more of Rochford's history, then your best course would be to join the Rochford Hundred Historical Society. This seeks to promote knowledge of the history of the area and would welcome your membership.

Introduction

Early Beginnings

Rochford is essentially an agricultural settlement. Its roots go back to the days of pre-history when it was peopled with primitive tribes who had migrated from the Continent. They settled close to the Essex seaboard where they were able to fish as well as hunt for their food. The Southend Museums display many objects from the Paleolithic, Mesolithic, Neolithic, Bronze and Early Iron Ages found at Rochford, including tools, weapons and burial urns. From time to time the ground yields evidence of early burials of these tribes.

The Bronze Age also brought the Beaker-folk to the area from that part of the Continent between the Baltic and the Rhine. These people insisted on having their treasured beakers buried with them, by their heads, for use in the next world. Sometime before the arrival of the Beaker-folk in Essex, the Kimmerians had wandered across from the edge of the Baltic and were joined by their kinsmen, the Kelts. They all took up residence in subterranean passages close to the Essex coast. They lived in perpetual darkness in underground caves with the males occasionally emerging at night to fish and hunt for food. Evidence of the remains of a Kimmerian village was found in Little Wakering 100 years ago.

The powerful *Trinovantes* tribe which dominated Essex when Caesar invaded Britain in 55/54 B.C. built up a good relationship with the Romans. There is considerable evidence of Roman settlement in the Rochford area. Roman villas, farmsteads, shops and pavements all exist under the ground in Rochford's town centre. We are indebted to the Romans for the embankments they built to keep out the sea. For four centuries the Romans held sway but in the year A.D. 420 they left Britain for good, leaving its people unprepared for war and unable to cope with any potential enemies. Consequently the next invaders, the Picts and Scots, completely ravaged the country until in A.D. 449 the Saxons were invited in to put a stop to these incursions. They did so, most successfully, and decided to stay but it was not until A.D. 527 that the Saxons finally took possession of Essex. Evidence of Saxon village settlements has been found in the Rochford area.

The Anglo-Saxons divided their territories into 'hundreds' each hundred consisting of a number of villages, their main purpose being to combat crime, violence and disorder and to bring about good rule and government. Each hundred was governed by 100 men. Their meetings were called hundred-moots, they met in the moot-hall in the chief town of the hundred (Rochford in this area) and their chairman was called the Hundred-man or Ealdorman. The Saxons had their own court known as the hundred-court and each hundred sent a representative to the court of the shire which was presided over by the Sheriff. The Sheriff, a man of power and importance, was ultimately responsible for good rule and government in his county.

Edgar the Peaceable, King of all the English, was responsible for establishing more firmly the hundreds under legislation known as The Ordinance of the Hundred in A.D. 973. This system of government by the hundreds continued over the years until by the last century Essex was divided into 14 hundreds. One of the largest was Rochford Hundred, embracing all the parishes from the south bank of the River Crouch to the sea and from Canvey, Benfleet and Rawreth in the west to Foulness and the interesting archipelago of islands in the east.

Towards the end of the last century the word 'hundred' was dropped from the title and was replaced by 'Union'. In 1895 the Unions were superceded by the Rural District Councils and the 27 parishes which formed successively the Rochford Hundred and the Rochford Union now became the Rochford Rural District Council. Not only did this council deal with day-to-day administration of local matters but, as agents for the Government, it had to cope with the effect of two World Wars on the population and severe flooding. In 1974, with the disbandment of rural district councils, the local authority became known as the Rochford District Council.

The Manors

The Manor of Rochford (Hall) is listed in Domesday Book, compiled for William the Conqueror in 1086, as follows:

Rochefort ten& Alured de . S . qđ teń . ı . lib hō . t . r . e . p . ꝩ . 7 p.
. ıı . hiđ . 7 . dim . Sep . v . uiłł . Tc . ıııı . bor . m̂ . xıı . Tc . ıı . ſer . m̂ . ııꞇ
tc . ıı . car in dnīo . m̂ . ııı . Tc . ııı . car . hom̂ . m̂ . ıııı . 7 . ı . lib hō
ten& . xxx . ac . 7 adhuc jacent huic mań . ıı . ac p̃ti . Silu . xx.
porc . ı . mol . Tc . ı . runc . 7 . vııı . porc . 7 . xı . ou . m̂ . ııı . runc . 7
. ıı . pułł . 7 . x . ań . 7 . xxı . porc . 7 . cLx . ou . 7 xxııı . ou . Tc ualuit
. c . ſoł . m̂ . vıı . lib.

Alfred holds Rochford from Swein, which 1 free man held before 1066 as a manor, for 2½ hides. Always 5 villagers. Then [1066] 4 smallholders, now 12; then 2 slaves, now 3. Then 2 ploughs in lordship, now 3. Then 3 men's ploughs, now 4.
1 free man holds 30 acres and they also lie in (the lands of) this manor. Meadow, 2 acres; woodland, 20 pigs; 1 mill. Then 1 cob, 8 pigs and 11 sheep; now 3 cobs, 2 foals, 10 cattle, 21 pigs, 160 sheep and 23 sheep.
Value then 100s; now £7.

Rochford Hall, standing near the west end of the parish church and now the home of Rochford Hundred Golf Club, was formerly the home of many noble families including the Earls of Ormond and Wiltshire, the family of Boleyn, Lord Rich, the Earls of Warwick and the Duke of Wellington. The original stone manor house was demolished and the mansion which took its place was built by James, Earl of Ormond, in the early 15th century. Some years later it was partly burned down as a result of lighted candles being left on the high altar in the private chapel.

Restored by Sir Thomas Boleyn, Lord of the Manor of Rochford and father of the ill-fated Anne, and considerably improved by Lord Rich, Lord Chancellor of England in Henry VIII's time, the Hall again suffered the ravages of fire in 1760 and remained for some time in a ruinous state. Eventually the Elizabethan windows were removed and modernised and the Tudor brickwork encased in plaster. Originally there were eight octagonal turrets, four in the inner angles of the building which housed spiral staircases of oak and four on the outer angles which were known as 'bowers'. Anne Boleyn sat and read in these bowers on fine days.

The mansion with its several courtyards stood in a large private park known as Rochford Park within the Great Forest of Essex. In its heyday it was noted for its lavish entertaining. The mansion played host to such notable personages as Henry VIII who courted Anne Boleyn here; the mother of Lord Bacon who 'learned more about God in the chapel at Rochford Hall than in 20 years of sermons in St Paul's Cathedral'; Sir Philip Sidney, the famous Elizabethan poet and soldier, lover of Penelope, first Countess of Warwick; and Oliver Cromwell whose daughter, Frances, by his wife Elizabeth Bouchier of nearby Little Stambridge Hall, married Lord Robert Rich, son of the third Earl of Warwick.

Lady Margaret Boleyn, wife of Sir William Boleyn of Blickling Hall, Norfolk, inherited the Rochford estates from her father, the last Earl of Ormond, whose full title was Sir Thomas Ormond de Rochford. Sir William Boleyn had a particular fondness for Rochford and with his wife resided here for many years until his death. Their grandchildren, Mary, George and Anne, children of Sir Thomas Boleyn and his wife, Elizabeth, were frequent visitors. Sir Thomas Boleyn was created Viscount Rochford in 1525 and his son, George, became Lord Rochford. Anne Boleyn is described by Henry VIII in several of his private documents as 'My Lady Anne of Rochford' and, in letters patent creating her Marquess of Pembroke, she is styled 'Lady Anne Rochford'. She was the first woman ever to be created a Marquess in her own right and took precedence over all others who had acquired that rank through marriage.

Anne's sister, Mary, who had married into the Somerset family of Carey, became Lord of the Manor of Rochford following her second marriage, this time to Sir William Stafford, when she inherited the estate after her father's death. She lived at Rochford Hall for many years with her second husband, and there she died. Her son, Henry Carey, Lord Hunsdon, had no interest in Rochford and sold the estate to Lord Rich of Hampshire. Hunsdon's grandson, also Henry, was created Viscount Rochford by James I.

From this family descended Richard Rich, a lawyer, who entered Henry VIII's court and was made Solicitor General in 1533. He was one of the worst characters that ever darkened the pages of history. Ruthless, mischief-making, a plausible liar and a truckler in religion and politics, he succeeded in bringing to the gallows Anne Boleyn, Sir Thomas More, the saintly Dr. Fisher and the King's fifth wife, Catherine Howard. Honours and estates were heaped upon him by the King and the part he played in dissolving the monasteries and other religious houses brought him further wealth from the many treasures stored there. He was created Lord Chancellor of England and Baron Rich of Lees. He lived and died at Rochford Hall. His funeral procession from Rochford to Felsted where he was interred was the most splendid ever seen in Essex. By letters patent dated 1618 the Lords Rich were created successive Earls of Warwick.

Rochford Hall passed through the hands of various owners and fell into a state of dereliction until put into good order by James Tabor, the last lord of the manor, at the turn of the present century, when the Hall became a typical Essex farmhouse. The north side of the Hall was acquired by Rochford Hundred Golf Club and the western end remained as a farmer's residence until 1981, when that also passed to the Golf Club.

In earlier times the mansion had a moat and was approached by a roadway through the park commencing near the old Rectory. In the park was an area known until the end of the 19th century as 'The Wilderness' and described as 'a beautiful retreat well stocked with noble thorn bushes'. The pretty brook flowing through The Wilderness was crossed only by stepping stones until a rustic bridge was built over it in 1897 to commemorate Queen Victoria's Diamond Jubilee. Seats were placed along Hall Road (formerly 'the Avenue') at strategic points to enable the public to sit and admire the pastoral scene across the park. The site of the manorial windmill was on rising ground north-east of Rochford behind the former Court House in South Street. Here for 600 years the Rochford millers ground their corn until the last mill was removed from there to Stambridge early in the 19th century.

In the grounds of Rochford Hall was a circular dove-cote, dating from Tudor times. Essex had only two Tudor dove-houses, one here at Rochford and the other at Writtle. The Rochford structure was built in 1540 and stood in the stack yard. It was erected by the express wish of Mary Boleyn, Anne's sister, when she inherited the manorial rights. This unique dove-cote was of red brick and thatch and considerably enhanced the grounds of Rochford Hall for well over three centuries until 1888 when, during a bad thunderstorm which hit the town, it was struck by lightning and caught alight. It was damaged beyond repair and had to be demolished.

A most interesting story concerning the birds of this dove-house is related by a Mrs. Witham of Rayleigh, aunt of Mrs. Violet Whittingham of Rochford. Mrs. Witham's father kept the *Horse and Groom Inn* in South Street, Rochford (formerly in Eastwood before a change of boundary), and it was there that the tithes of Eastwood were paid at the inn parlour. A tithe dinner would be held at six in the evening. The main dish would be an enormous pigeon pie, the birds for this being brought by the old shepherd from the dove-cote at Rochford Hall in his roomy side pockets the evening before. Mrs. Witham remembered the old gentleman taking the birds one by one from the depths of his pockets. This ancient custom of paying the tithes has long since died out but the tithe dinner and its pigeon pie at the *Horse and Groom* was for many years a great occasion in the life of this historic market town.

The manor house of *Doggetts* is situated to the north-east of Rochford with its grounds extending into Little Stambridge. Situated in a peaceful location and clad for many years in ivy and other creepers, the present-day residence is one of the most attractive in this hundred. Its well-kept lawns and gardens are greatly admired. There are several cottages on the estate. One with a thatched roof stood for many years in an old-world garden at the side of the Bobbing Pond, an ornamental lake studded with islands. Here, local witches were ducked into the water while seated on a stool, their heads bobbing up between duckings.

Doggetts takes its name from Robert Doggett who resided here c.1305 and whose descendants held the manor for several centuries. In 1619 Doggetts came into the possession of the Earl of Warwick and remained in the hands of the Rochford manorial lord until it was sold in 1867 to William Taylor Meeson, a Shropshire man. Meeson was resident at Doggetts and worked the farm for over half a century. It was he who gave the name Romney Marsh to the meadow adjoining the Bobbing Pond as he always purchased sheep from Romney Marsh in Kent. They were brought by rail to Rochford Station and placed in the Romney Marsh meadow at Doggetts to rest for a day or two after the journey.

The Lawless or Whispering Court

King's Hill, situated in East Street, Rochford, with a flank frontage to Old Ship Lane, stands cheek-by-jowl with the enchanting King's Hill Cottage. Both properties date from the 14th century, though the house has later additions and a modern extension to the north. Both buildings are filled with mellow timber beams and open brick fireplaces.

Their grounds are extensive. For three centuries the Lawless or Whispering Court was held in the garden in front of the house. Before that it was held at Rayleigh, accessible only by a muddy track. No one knows exactly when this court was instituted or by whom but a process of elimination suggests Lord Ewyas of Wales who was Lord of the Manor here around 1136. His tenants were annoyed by the lord's long absences from Rochford, as he was never present to hear their grievances and disputes over land. They were determined to rectify this and secretly plotted against him as they awaited his return after months of absence. He arrived at the Hall late one night. He retired to his chamber to sleep and at midnight was woken by the crowing of a barnyard cockerel and overheard loud whispers coming from the courtyard below. His tenants, cloaked and hooded with daggers concealed beneath their garments, were plotting to murder him. He strode out into the courtyard, reprimanded them for their treachery and, as penance, commanded them to assemble round a specially-made post at King's Hill, Rayleigh, annually on the Wednesday after Michaelmas to do homage for their lands in a whisper.

The court was held at Rayleigh for several centuries until the 2nd Earl of Warwick decided it would be more convenient to have the court transferred to Rochford. The new site at Rochford was then given the original name of King's Hill and the Whispering Post erected in front of the house, where it stands to the present day. It is five feet high and made of wood. Its top is wrought with mouldings and finishes in a sharp pyramid. It is shaped like a candle with wick and flame. The deeds of King's Hill stipulate that this post must never be removed and must be renewed as and when necessary.

Preceeding the court, a supper was provided at the *King's Head Inn* in Rochford market place by the lord of the manor, the bill of fare being the same each year – boiled fowls with vegetables, leg of mutton with caper sauce, ale, plum pudding, apple tart and sweets. After supper, there was singing, talking and mugs of steaming sweet punch. At midnight the inebriated tenants made their way to King's Hill, crossing the market place, along Market Alley, down Old Ship Lane and then through the field gate in East Street. Once round the post the steward would summon the tenants to the court in a low voice like a whisper, and then by lantern light would call the names of the persons owing suit and service to the court, concluding with the following proclamation:

> Oh yes, oh yes, oh yes, all persons who have appeared at this court for the manor of King's Hill have leave to depart hence keeping their day and hour on a new summons. God save the King.

By the end of the last century the Whispering Court had become a riotous affair with local boys carrying flaming firebrands and crowing lustily. Onlookers came from far and wide, and the market square would become crowded with people. The locals threw their flaming firebrands into a heap in the middle of the market place and chanted the Song of the Lawless Court. The owners of property round the market place became alarmed, the town crier rang his bell loud and long calling to everyone to disperse but to no avail. The turn of the century saw the departure of many of the manorial lords and with them went their courts and many other interesting customs of a bygone age.

The Earls of Rochford

Besides Sir Thomas Boleyn, Anne's father, the town gave the title of Earl of Rochford to the Nassau family from Holland who served this country with distinction. They were descended from Frederick de Nassau, a natural son of Henry de Nassau, Prince of Orange and grandfather to King William III. Frederick de Nassau was granted the lordship of Zuyleistein in Holland and assumed that surname. His son, William Henry de Zuyleistein, was cousin and confidante of William of Orange and accompanied him to England when he ascended the throne as William III to rule jointly with his wife and cousin, Mary II. At the battle of Landen in 1693, de Nassau, severely wounded and ultimately taken prisoner, rescued the King when he was surrounded by the enemy and in great danger. For these services to the monarch he was granted the Earldom of Rochford. William III's death in 1695 was a bitter blow to him and he returned to Holland for good, dying in Zuyleistein in 1708. His eldest son, William Henry de Nassau Zuyleistein, succeeded him as the second Earl of Rochford. He fought under Marlborough and was the bearer of despatches announcing the victory of Blenheim in 1704 where he had command of part of the English army. Unmarried, he was succeeded by his brother Frederick, 3rd Earl of Rochford, who married Bessie Savage, daughter of Lord Rivers. Through her he obtained the estates at St Osyth, Essex, as well as St Osyth's Priory. His elder son, William Henry, succeeded to the title and this Earl, while living at the Priory, brought from Italy the first Lombardy poplars which can still be seen in the park today. In 1756 he was commissioned Lord Lieutenant of Essex and *Custos Rotulorum*. At the time of George II's death he was Groom of the Stole and as such was entitled to the furniture of the room in which the King died. For many years His Majesty's death bed quilt did duty as an altar cloth at St Osyth's parish church.

The Earl's nephew, William Henry, succeeded him as 5th Earl of Rochford. He spent most of his life at the manor house in Easton, Suffolk, another of the family estates. He died in 1830, unmarried. The estate at St Osyth's went to Frederic Nassau, a natural son of the 4th Earl, while those at Easton passed to the 5th Earl's maternal cousin, the 10th Duke of Hamilton, and the Earldom of Rochford became extinct.

The Market Square, Streets and Shops

Originally, there were two market places built in Rochford by medieval planners based on their formula of 'a Square for God and a Square for man'. Only one now remains and it is almost as closed as an Italian Piazza. This market square was the scene of the martyrdom of John Simson. In 1555 the clergy, on Queen Mary's instructions, had been told to note any parishioners who refused to conform to the Roman Catholic Church. Simson and his friend, Ardeley, both simple farm labourers working at Great Wigborough, had refused to conform and on trial were found guilty, following the example of many humble people who refused to change their religion and so met their death by burning at the stake. These public burnings did not take place in their home village as it was feared such an action would lead to rioting. Ardeley was led to his death in Rayleigh High Street while Simson was thrown into the flames on a funeral pyre in Rochford Square, his hands chained behind him to the stake. A memorial tablet to Simson can be found on the wall of the baker's shop in Market Alley.

The market for the sale of livestock was the brain-child of Sir Guy de Rochford in 1247 and continued successfully for about four centuries. Captain Harriot of Stambridge revived it in the 18th century and it continued as a cattle market until 1959 when it closed 'for good'. However, the 1960s saw yet another revival and with a great flourish it re-opened as a general market and has continued to thrive ever since.

In earlier centuries the Square used to have interesting buildings on all four sides but in the late 1960s the whole of the east side was pulled down to make way for a supermarket and a handful of modern shops and offices. Down came Shelley's grocery store, Soper's greengrocery and the little cottages which did duty as a tailor's shop and a tea-room. The earthquake of 1884 and the fire at the oil store soon after damaged the shops on the north side. Some of these, including the saddlers, were demolished one Sunday morning in 1968 to make way for a new shop and the village library. On the west side the elegant Connaught House has weathered the ravages of time but the adjoining cottage 'Fernbank' was demolished in recent years to make way for the National Westminster Bank. On the south side the buildings are of even greater interest. The Women's Institute Hall, built in mid-Victorian times as a corn exchange on the site of an old inn, the *Vernon's Head* (formerly the *Post Boy*), has served in turn as a laundry, a garage for motor repairs and a community centre where village concerts and similar gatherings were held.

Barclays Bank was built in 1853 as the bank of Sparrow, Round, Green, Tufnell and Round. Barclays took it over in 1866. The *King's Head* next door served as the mecca of farmers on market days. Many a deal was struck over the bar counter here. The *King's Head* is the most historic of all the towns's inns. The Rochford stage-coach ran from this inn to Aldgate High Street and back from 1700 to the end of the last century. Inside passengers were charged 8 shillings fare and outside 4 shillings.

In the centre of the Square was an ancient market house, built in 1707, which for many years at the turn of the last century housed the village fire engine, pigs and a barber's shop. The railings used at the weekly market were kept upstairs where wool was weighed. The market house eventually fell into dilapidation and had to be demolished in 1861. Nearby was the parish pump which supplied the whole village with water at one-farthing a pailful. This was superseded by a horse-drawn water cart which carried water from Southend to be sold at one-halfpenny a pailful. The needs of the animals were not overlooked as a fountain and horse trough were built in the Square to commemorate the accession of Edward VII in 1901. The sweep's horse, 'Rhubub', was the last to make use of this and on his death the fountain and trough were moved to Hockley Woods where they are still in daily use.

Streets and Roads

North, South, East and West Streets meet at the crossroads which lead into the market square. West Street was formerly known as Church Street (or Station Road) and South Street as High Street.

One enters the town from Southend at the Salt Bridge. There has been a bridge on this site since 1777. Prior to that there was a deep ford. When work on the construction of the by-pass (Bradley Way) began in 1967, a new and larger bridge was planned to take the heavy traffic load. During the subsequent demolition of Salt Bridge, the 1772 bridge was uncovered. This consisted of three spans of arches, hitherto unknown, but similar to the arch by the railway bridge (the Clappe Gate), built in 1777.

South Street is noted for its Georgian-fronted residences – the house of the local doctors, the Manse and the Red House, all now used as civic offices. The Red House was formerly occupied by Mr. and Mrs. Hugh Rankin. One of their grand-children recalls a time during the 1914-18 war when a cow, being driven from the market along South Street, entered Red House via the coach house and kitchen door and had to be driven down the front steps, though not before it had run into the drawing-room and ruined the expensive carpet!

George Wood, a solicitor, lived next door to the Old House and in the garden planted a large variety of rare shrubs and plants. The Old House is a delightful example of a 13th-century timber-framed house which has lately undergone major restoration. Over the centuries it was used as a private dwelling and in the 18th century it contained shop premises. It is now used as civic offices. On the east side of South Street can be seen the Old Court House, erected in 1859 to house the County Court until new premises were built in Southend in the 1930s. In the Old Court House is an ancient well, several feet deep, at the foot of the entrance staircase. A stream of clear water runs beneath the building. Used as offices by the Rochford Rural District Council until 1974, the Court House was then sold to the Freemasons as a masonic temple.

The old fire station, now a pretty cottage, can be found in North Street opposite the site where once stood the village smithy. The first post office was housed in a thatched cottage behind the present *Rose and Crown* car park. It was later transferred to West Street where the old post-box can still be seen in the wall of an ancient house. The Police Station, formerly in North Street, was moved to its present position in South Street during the First World War, the post office taking over their former premises in North Street which still contains the police cells below. At the rear of this post office, in Bishop's Lane, once stood the candle factory.

Passing through the market square via Market Alley, one comes to West Street where there are some small, very charming old-world shops in cottage premises. Arthur Harrington was the chemist there 100 years ago. Normally, tooth extraction was carried out by a travelling dentist who plied his trade at markets and fairs taking with him his chair in which would sit the patient while all and sundry looked on as the operation proceeded. Arthur Harrington, the chemist, would deal with those needing more urgent treatment by extracting teeth for a fee at the back of his shop, now occupied by the Co-op Chemist. Harrington employed a young boy to drag the unfortunate victims into the back yard to help them to 'come round' after fainting. The experience of dental extraction must have been terrifying and painful in an age when few, if any, anaesthetics were used.

East Street and Palmer's Corner contained a few shops and an auctioneer's but otherwise was mainly residential, the most interesting property apart from King's Hill being Fir Tree House and the adjoining cottage. The house was for several generations the home of the village veterinary surgeon, named Sparrow. Built on varying levels and in perfect condition, the former veterinary surgery and waiting room now comprise a charming lounge looking out upon one of the most beautiful landscaped gardens in Rochford.

Inns

The town boasts many very pleasant and historic inns including the *Old Ship*, the *New Ship*, the *Marlborough Head*, the *King's Head*, the *Anne Boleyn*, the *Rose and Crown*, the *White Horse* and the *Golden Lion*. The *Old Ship*, which stands in North Street, had for many years iron rings on the outer wall to which fairground attendants would tether their performing bears on fair and market days while they themselves partook of a mug of ale. The upstairs room was the lodge room of Rochford's True Friendship Lodge of Freemasons in the last century and the meeting place of Rochford's Memnonian Society (Music Club).

* * * * *

Today, Rochford is a thriving market town with a busy airport within its boundaries. It is surrounded by a group of historic villages: Stambridge with its strong American connections; Eastwood with its beautiful 380-year-old manor-house of 'Cockethurst';

Sutton with its church which has the finest chancel arch in Essex; Canewdon, an old-world village of shepherds, marshes, farmworkers and barge-sailors; Ashingdon, where Ironside met the conqueror, Canute, at the Battle of Assandune; and Paglesham, a tiny village of quiet beauty and infinite peace with two inns, the *Punch Bowl* and the *Plough and Sail*, low-ceilinged, ancient and snug where many a smuggling plot was hatched at dead of night. Beyond lies the sea-country of Foulness and its satellite islands, a kingdom of crabs and curlews where mud flats stretch for miles and the land melts into the sea.

1. Chapman and André's map of Essex, 1777.

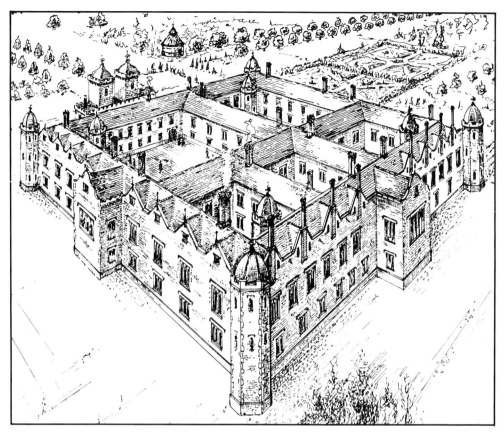

2. A conjectural drawing by N. H. Barnes of Rochford Hall, based on the early foundations and showing the mansion and dove-cote in Tudor times.

3. Rochford Hall showing the west wing in the 18th century.

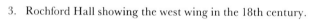

4. Rochford Hall at the turn of the present century.

5. Rochford Hall, *c*.1920.

6.   Old barn at Rochford, 1964.

7.   The Tudor kitchen at Rochford Hall, *c.*1930.

8. Doggetts, Rochford.

9. King's Hill, Rochford, showing the Whispering Post in the foreground.

10. King's Hill at the turn of the century.

11.   King's Hill in the 1920s.

12.   (*left*) King's Hill: the Whispering Post shaped like a candle round which the Whispering Court would gather annually to do homage for their lands in a whisper.

13.   (*above*) King's Hill, the hall.

14. The first of the Earls of Rochford whose estates were in St Osyth, Essex, and Easton, Suffolk. The coachman to the last Earl was George Girdler who died in 1853 and whose great grand-daughter, Mrs. Thora Morley, lives in Sutton Road, Rochford, today. On the old coachman's tomb in Easton churchyard is this inscription: 'For 43 years a faithful servant and coachman to the late Earl of Rochford'.

FAITHFUL UNTO DEATH
REV.II.10

TO THE GLORY OF GOD
AND
IN THANKFUL MEMORY OF
JOHN SIMSON
A NATIVE OF GREAT WIGBOROUGH,
ESSEX
WHO WAS BURNT AT THE STAKE
AT OR NEAR THIS MARKET PLACE
ON JUNE 10TH 1555
FOR HIS
PROTESTANT
CONVICTIONS.

15.   Commemorative plaque on the wall of the bakery in Market Alley off the Market Square to John Simson, burnt at the stake in the Square in 1555.

16.   The Market Square looking north-east, *c.*1800. The market house was demolished in 1861.

17.   An early photograph of Rochford Market Square showing the former market house built in 1707. The town bell hung in the bell cote.

18.   South side of Market Square with the *King's Head* on the extreme right, *c.*1860.

19.   Market Square. A great fire broke out on July 1884 in an oil store to the left of the picture and destroyed all the buildings on the north side of the Square.

20. Mr. Goodman, the saddler, standing outside his shop in Market Square, *c.*1890.

21. Market Square before mechanisation, looking south-west and showing (left to right) the *King's Head*, Barclay's Bank, the Corn Exchange which was built in 1866 (now the Women's Institute), 'Nanny' Carter's clock shop and Connaught House.

22. This 1910 picture shows the former elegance of the Market Square, now lost because of the large volume of traffic using it as a car park.

23. The town pump in the Market Square from which villagers used to collect water at one-farthing a pail. The boy standing by the post in this 1910 photograph was named Kemp.

24. Horse-drawn water supply cart from Southend selling water at one half-penny a pail, *c*.1880.

25. North side of Market Square showing the saddler's shop, an adjoining cottage, the market offices and the old town pump, *c*.1890.

26.   The local newsagent waits for his pail to fill at the town pump, *c.*1920.

27. Local horses queueing up for a drink at their old trough in Market Square, *c*.1910.

28. Old cottages on the east side of Market Square just prior to demolition in the 1960s.

29. The most elegant building in Market Square is Connaught House on the left. Built in 1769 by Cottis as a result of a fortunate lottery ticket, it was the private residence successively of solicitors, Vanderzee, Comport and Gregson and in this century of a Mr. Halsey who married Phyllis Rankin of Broomhills, Stambridge. It is today used as offices by Essex County Council.

30. Market Square, *c*.1910: the Ancient Order of Foresters, Rochford Branch.

31.   Re-opening of Rochford cattle market in Market Square in 1914.

32.   Another view of market day, *c*.1912.

33. Townsfolk celebrating the end of the First World War in Market Square.

34. Rochford cattle market during the Second World War.

35. North-east corner of the Market Square, *c.*1920, with the Salvation Army in full song.

36. The crossroads at Palmer's corner. The entrance to North Street is on the left. Palmer's corner accommodated the auctioneer's office, and in the background the *New Ship Inn* can be seen in East Street. Note the old man playing his violin in the middle of the road. Today this is the central point of the one-way traffic system in the busy town. This photograph was taken about 1880.

37. At the crossroads, *c.*1955, showing Soper's greengrocery shop (*right*) and Shelley's grocery (*left*) before the advent of the supermarket.

38. Salt Bridge, South Street, before the bypass was constructed in 1967.

39. South Street, formerly High Street, looking towards the crossroads when the road was just a muddy track around 1920. The cart is waiting outside the *Horse and Groom Inn*. Horner's meadow is on the left. This was absorbed into the bypass in 1967.

40. Another view of the High Street looking towards the crossroads, *c.*1910.

41. South Street from the crossroads looking towards Southend. The Manse, built in 1706, is on the left.

42. Garden at the rear of the County Court, *c.*1890. The Old People's Day Centre now occupies this site.

43. South Street with the old County Court on the left, built in 1859. The building is now a Masonic Temple.

44.   The west side of South Street close to Back Lane.

45.   The same view with the late Jessie Payne's uncle, Mr. Golding, the owner of the house, in the doorway with his dog. The house was demolished in about 1956. Arthy's bakery can be seen on the corner of Back Lane.

46. Georgian-fronted houses on the east side of South Street. From left to right, the Manse (residence of the Congregational church minister), the hairdresser's and Roche House, home of the local doctor.

47. The east side of South Street in 1963. From left to right, the hairdresser's, Roche House and Red House.

48. Red House, South Street: Mrs. Hugh Rankin's staff with Tom Purkiss, the butler, in the background, *c.*1895.

49. South Street with the Old House on the left and, next to it, George Wood's house with the wheelwright's shop adjoining. On the right behind the lamp post is Sydenham House, once a boarding school.

50. The Old House, South Street, formerly Tudor House. This 13th-century timber-framed building has now been restored.

51. The Old House, South Street: the side aspect before restoration.

52. Sydenham House Boarding School, South Street, *c*.1880.

53. South Street looking towards Southend with the *Horse and Groom* on the right.

54. Old cottages in North Street.

55.   Market Alley, formerly Elcock's Alley and Cocker's Alley, leading to Market Square from North Street. Mr. Fulcher's grandfather is standing in the foreground. The old cottage on the right has now been replaced by a shoe shop and that on the left by a bakery. This photograph was taken around 1900.

56. North Street showing the entrance to the *Old Ship Inn* on the right, *c*.1910.

57. The *Old Ship Inn*, *c*.1929.

58. The old post office in North Street which dates from around 1835.

59. View of North Street facing south with Rochford post office in premises formerly occupied by the Police Station.

60. Ash Tree Cottage, North Street, *c.*1915. This building stood in front of the Congregational church but has now been demolished.

61. Mr. Potter's general stores in North Street, 1909.

62.   The smithy in North Street, opposite the *White Horse Inn*. Mr. Hubert Bacon is shoeing while his father stands by. This photograph was taken *c*.1930.

63. East Street looking towards Stambridge with Fir Tree House, residence of the village veterinary surgeon for many generations, on the right.

64. In earlier days, the veterinary surgeons did their rounds in a horse and cart. This shows their faithful stallion, Jubilee Jock, with his groom, Fred Watson, in the grounds of King's Hill, East Street.

65. Three generations of veterinary surgeons in the same family, 1948. Henry Foster Sparrow (*left*), his son, Captain
H. D. Sparrow (*right*), his grandson, Leonard Sparrow (*centre*), with young Michael, his great grandson, now a Squadron-
Leader in the Royal Air Force.

66. West Street 30 years ago with the *Marlborough Head* on the right at the entrance to Back Lane.

67. The old watermill cottage, West Street. The mill stream ran from Romney Marsh across the hospital site to West Street.

68. Corn Exchange Garage, West Street, now the Women's Institute.

69.   West Street, *c.*1920. Willan's grocery shop was a well-known landmark in the village. Note the fine trees at the entrance to Back Lane behind the horse and cart. Rochford Cycle Co. had the shop at the corner. The white house on the right was occupied successively by the Sorrell and Carter families.

70. West Street, with Barclays Bank on the left and the Women's Institute (formerly a corn exchange, laundry and garage) adjoining.

71. The blacksmith's forge in West Street.

72.   Shops in West Street. 'The Hollies', an 18th-century house on the middle-left, has shop premises adjoining. Arthur Harrington's chemist's shop can be seen in the background on the left.

73.   Another view of 'The Hollies', West Street. At the turn of the century the shop premises were used as the Rate Collector's office.

74. The post office, West Street, with Mr. J. Francis, postmaster and printer, at the door, *c.*1890.

75. West Street from Market Square.

76. West Street in 1908.

77. Station Road (now West Street), looking towards the town, with the entrance to Station Approach on the right.

78. The coming of the railway to Rochford was an occasion of rejoicing for the town. The line was extended from Wickford to Southend in 1889, stations erected and a goods shed put up close to the line in Rochford. This picture shows the stationmaster's house with the railway offices in the background.

79. An early view of the railway taken from the station platform at the Hall Road entrance.

80. Rochford reservoir, close to the station, contained the water necessary for the working of the steam engines. This area has now been landscaped and the reservoir is a beautiful lake surrounded by parkland.

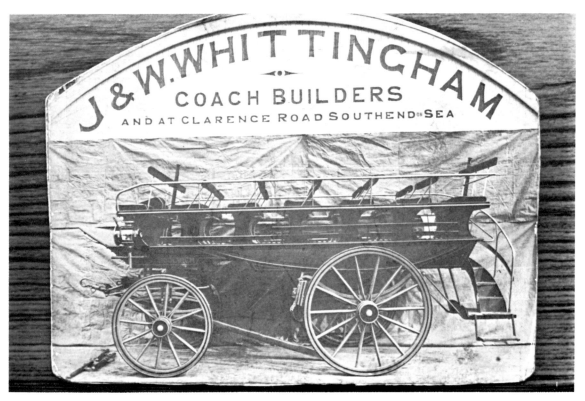

81. J. & W. Whittingham, coach builders from 1800. The motor engineering business has been in the Whittingham family since 1900 and is run by Mark, David and Robert Whittingham today. The Whittinghams, who originated from Long Melford, Suffolk, are Rochford's oldest family.

82. Station Road, looking west, with Whittingham's coach building works on the right.

83. Station Road was that section of West Street from Union Lane westwards to its junction (known as the Clappe Gate) with Ashingdon Road and Hall Road (formerly The Avenue). On the left are some of the almshouses built by Lord Rich in the early 17th century. On the right is the Ironwell which flows through fields to Hawkwell along Ironwell Lane.

84. The Avenue at the turn of the century with Rochford Park on the left. Today it is Hall Road.

85. The Avenue. Seats were erected on the west side to enable the public to relax and admire the splendid view across the Park to the Wilderness.

86. London Road at the turn of the century, with the old *Cock Inn* on the right. Today this is Hall Road.

87. Ironwell Lane. For centuries this was the main thoroughfare to London along which the stage-coaches passed, travelling from Aldgate to the *King's Head*, Rochford.

88. Dalys Road before Rochford hospital was erected, *c*.1920.

89. The old workhouse, Southend Road. This dates from about 1750.

90. Rochford Union workhouse. This was erected in 1837 and replaced all parish workhouses.

91. An aerial view of Rochford General Hospital, showing the old workhouse buildings, still in use, with the modern hospital and nurses' home.

THE SCHOOL, ROCHFORD.

92. Rochford School in centre background, known today as Rochford Junior School, with the National Schoolroom (now St Andrew's parish hall) on the right. The rector is standing on the bridge which was built in 1777. This road junction was known as the Clappe Gate in earlier times.

93. Ashingdon Road leading to the *Victory Inn, c.*1920.

94.   Rochford's Band of Hope, *c*.1900.

95. Weir Pond Road, looking towards North Street.

96. Weir Pond Road, looking towards Stambridge.

97. The weir pond.

98. Custom House, Weir Pond Road.

99. The Dalys Road/Ashingdon Road junction early this century. In this cottage lived George Hart and Mr. and Mrs. Facey; the men were farm hands for Meeson's.

100. Southend Road near the junction with Queen Elizabeth Chase, *c.*1918. Today this is the busy main road linking Rochford with Southend.

101. Rochford Road leading to Prittlewell village, *c.*1870. The bridge crosses Prittle Brook which flows through the fields to Sutton.

102. Sutton Road, Rochford. Sutton Ford Bridge over Prittle Brook, *c*.1890.

103. Winter at Sutton Corner, 1974.

104. Sutton church, Rochford. Built in the Norman period, it was heavily restored in 1869. The chancel arch is a masterpiece of the Norman builders, still boasting its original medieval paint.

105. Sutton church interior at harvest-time.

106. The exquisite regency memorial to Chester Moor Hall, inventor of the achromatic lens, at Sutton church.

107.   Rochford parish church of St Andrew's, south aspect. Largely 15th-century, the tower was added in 1515 by the last Earl of Ormond, Anne Boleyn's maternal grandfather, who lived nearby at Rochford Hall.

108.   St Andrew's from the west.

109.   St Andrew's church and lychgate.

110.   An early interior view of Rochford parish church.

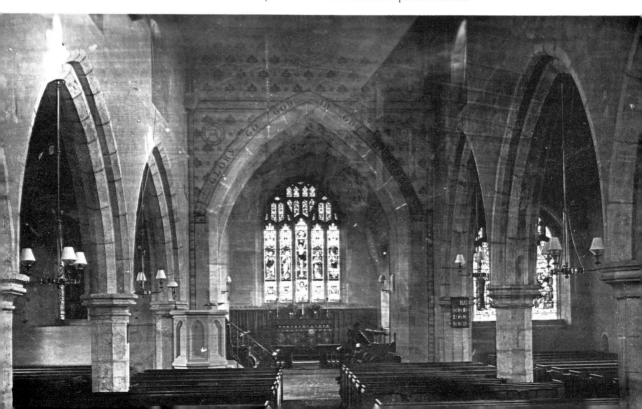

111. & 112.   A Rochford murder which excited much interest. In 1853 Emma Hart was murdered and her body thrown into the brook which flows through the Wilderness by Rochford parish church. The photograph above shows the scene of the murder and the one below shows a group of men searching for the murder weapon. Emma Hart's grave is in Rochford churchyard.

113. Rochford Congregational chapel, North Street, built in 1741.

114. Rochford Methodist church. The Methodists' first church was erected in 1822 near the Market Square. Nineteen years later they moved to North Street next to the hospital side entrance. In 1880 they built their present church on Chapel Field in North Street.

1851.

THE WESLEYAN METHODIST PLAN

OF THE MALDON CIRCUIT.

PLACES AND TIME.		FEB. 2	9	16	23	MAR. 2	9	16	23	30	APR. 6	13	20	27
MALDON	10½	1	20	1 u	7	1 t	5	2 c	1	3	1	1	18	1 c
	3	9	20	10 u	5	1 l	19	a c	22	3	21	17	18	5 c
	6	4	1 s	3 u	1	1	19	2 c	22	1 s	21	1	7	2 c
Tuesday	7	1	1	1	1	1	1	2 m	1	5	1	1	1	2 m
Goldhanger	2½	10	17	1 c	9	13	3	20	1	7 c	10	19	17	9 c
	6	10	17	1 c	9	13	3	20	1 s	7 c	10	19	17	9 c
Wednesday	6½	1		1		1 t		1		1		1		1
Totham	10½	19	1 s	5 u	20	17	7 c	13	3	9	15	10	5	2 c
	2½	19		5 u	20	17	7 c	13	3	9	15	10	5	2 c
Wednesday	6½		1		1		1 t		1		1		1	
Latchingdon	10½	3	15	4	1 c	10	13	9	7	1 c	3	15	9	7 c
	2½	3	15	4	1 c	10	13	9	7	1 c	3	15	9	7 c
Friday	6½	.	1					1 s				1		
Ostend	10½	15	3	7	2 u	4	1 t	5	10 c	15	2	9	1 c	15
Burnham	2½	12	3	7	2 u	4	1	5	10 c	16	2	9	1 c	8
	6½	12	3	7	2 u	4	1 s	5	10 c	16	2	9	1 c	8
Monday	7				2		1				2		1	
Leigh	10½	2	2	12 u	6	2	2	6	2 c	2	14	2	11 c	16
	2½	6	•	14 u	p	11	2	6	12 c	•	14	2	11 c	16
	6½	6	2 l	2 u	6	11	2	1 s	12 c	11	6	2	2 c	16
Tuesday	7	2		2		2		1 m		2	2	2		1 m
Rochford	10½	16	p	2 u	14	•	15	1	16	12 c	•	6	2	12 c
	2½	2	11	2 u	14	2	15	1 s	11	2 c	12	6	2	12 c
	6½	2	11	12 u	12	2 l	6	12	11	2 c	12	6	12	1 c
Tuesday	6½		2		2	2		2			2		2	
Rayleigh	10½	11	p	11 c	p	12	p	11	p	6	p	14	p	11 c
	2½	•	14	6 c	16	12	14	•	2 c	6	16	14	•	6 c
	6½	11	14	6 c	16	12	14	11	2 c	6	16	14	11	6 c
Thursday	6½	2		2		2	-	2		2		2		2
Hadleigh	2½	14	2 u	16	11	14	11	16 c	6	14	11	16	6 c	14
	6½	14	6 u	16	11	14	11	16 c	6	14	11	16	6 c	14
Wednesday	6½	2		2		2		2		2	2		2	
The Basin	6½	1				3					1			

PREACHERS.

1. WEST, *Maldon*
2. REACHER, *Leigh*
3. Stratford, *Maldon*
4. Harland, *Maldon*
5. King, *Maldon*
6. Tomlin, *Leigh*
7. Freeman, *Maldon*
8. Cotgrove, *Leigh*
9. Sutton, *Maldon*
10. Juniper, *Heybridge*
11. Frost, *Rayleigh*
12. M'Durmid, *Rochford*
13. Crowe, *Totham*

EXHORTERS.

14. Osborne, *Leigh*
15. Argent, *Burnham*
16. Shepherd, *Rochford*
17. Chaplin, *Totham*

From the CHELMSFORD CIRCUIT.

18. Leech, *Chelmsford*
19. Aves, *Hatfield*
20. Bearman, *Hatfield*
21. Coleman, sen., *Chelmsford*
22. Coleman, jun., *Chelmsford*

REFERENCES.

s. Sacrament
l. Lovefeast
c. Circuit collection
u. United Chapel, and Wesleyan Education Fund Collection
t. Tickets
m. Monday
p. Prayer Meeting

The Quarterly Meeting will be held at ROCHFORD, on Tuesday, April the 1st.—The Local Preachers to meet at 2 and the Stewards at 3 o'clock.—The Quarterly Fast is on Friday, March 28th.

EVERY PREACHER IS EXPECTED TO TAKE HIS OWN APPOINTMENT, OR PROCURE AN ACCREDITED SUBSTITUTE.

The Stewards are requested to make the collections on the days appointed, and get them published the preceding Sabbaths.

Wesleyan Hymn Books, Magazines, and other Religious Publications may be ordered through the Ministers at Maldon and Leigh.

Marriages may be solemnized in the Chapel at Maldon.

[*Price 2d.*

115. Plan of the Maldon Methodist circuit in 1851, giving the arrangements for the Rochford church.

116. No. 3 Barrack Lane, Rochford, birthplace in 1800 of James Banyard, founder and first bishop of the Peculiar People. He held prayer meetings and services here and preached in the Market Square where he was pelted with refuse. This was the origin of the Union of Evangelical Free Churches. Rochford's Evangelical church today is in Rocheway.

117. James Banyard's house after his marriage, c.1840. This was in North Street.

118.   Rochford's refuse collection cart, *c.*1928.

119.   Rochford fire brigade outside the fire station, *c.*1928. The men were all local tradesmen and only part-time firemen. From left to right, S. Weavers (driver), B. Wallace, B. Potter, G. Ducker, H. Chapman. The bowler-hatted man was a retired London fire officer. The bell was formerly on H.M.S. *Canterbury.*

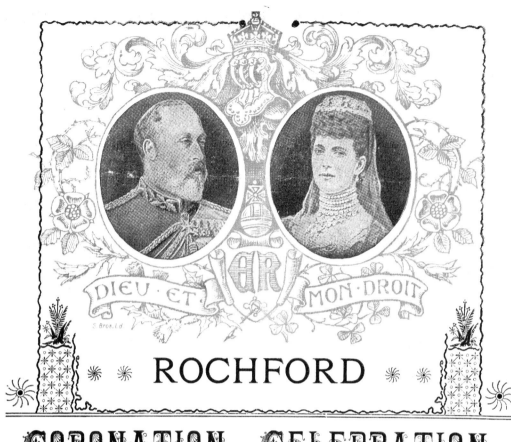

ROCHFORD

CORONATION CELEBRATION.

Thursday, 26th June,

1902.

PROGRAMME. = =

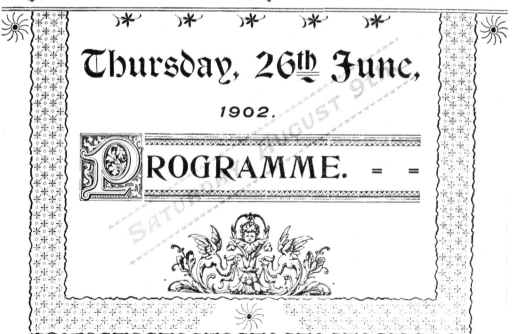

120.   Coronation of Edward VII, 1902. His Majesty was struck down with appendicitis so the coronation date had to be postponed from 26 June to 9 August to give him time to recover. This local programme shows the latter date superimposed over the original.

Programme

OF THE

PUBLIC REJOICINGS

TO BE HELD IN

ROCHFORD,

ON

WEDNESDAY, JUNE 22ND, 1887,

IN COMMEMORATION OF THE

Golden Anniversary of the Accession of

Her Most Gracious Majesty, Queen Victoria,

WHOM GOD PRESERVE.

J. FRANCIS AND SONS, STEAM PRINTERS, ROCHFORD AND SOUTHEND.

121. Queen Victoria's Golden Jubilee, 1887.

The Fifth Annual Meeting.

Rochford Park Races

WILL BE HELD

ON A MILE COURSE

Adjoining ROCHFORD LAWN,

ON

WEDNESDAY, AUGUST 23RD, 1899.

IN **£100** STAKES.

IN **£100** STAKES.

STEWARDS:—

MAJOR RASCH, M.P.,   Z. PETTITT, ESQ.,   H. DENNIS, ESQ.,

J. WALKER, ESQ.,   E. ROCHESTER, ESQ.,   A. C. W. HOBMAN, ESQ.

Judge:—S. S. BAKER, ESQ., J.P.,   Starter:—A. STALLIBRASS, ESQ.,

Clerk of the Scales:—G. F. GOLDING, ESQ.,

Clerk of the Course:—P. TRIGG, ESQ.,

Stake-holder:—H. WICKES, ESQ.,   Auctioneer:—W. V. WILLSON, ESQ.,

Veterinary Surgeon:—E. SPARROW, ESQ.

STATION:—ROCHFORD, G.E.R.   TELEGRAMS:—WALKER, ROCHFORD, ESSEX,

FRANCIS AND SONS, STEAM PRINTERS, ROCHFORD.

122.   Rochford Park Races. These were held on the course close to Rochford Hall from 1896 when advertisements announced it as 'The prettiest racecourse in England situated in the heart of a wood'. Later the course was transferred to Doggetts.

123. The racecourse at Doggetts was constructed in 1928 under the patronage of Lord Louth.

ROCHFORD
Cricket ✻ Club.

❧ DRAMATIC ❧

ENTERTAINMENT

IN THE

CORN EXCHANGE, ROCHFORD,

WEDNESDAY, APRIL 29th, 1896.

Reserved Seats, 2/-. . . .

. . . . Unreserved Seats, 1/-.

Promenade, 6d.

Tickets to be obtained of Mr. WRIGHT, Chemist, (Successor to Mr. HARRINGTON).

Doors open at 7·30.   Commence at 8.

CARRIAGES AT 10 P.M.

J.S.& E. 062

FRANCIS & SONS, STEAM PRINTERS, ROCHFORD.

124. Rochford Cricket Club programme of Dramatic Entertainment at the Corn Exchange, Rochford, 1896.

125. Rochford Cycling Club, *c*.1890.

126. Miss Mary Shelley, daughter of Shelley the grocer in Market Square, was a keen member of the local cycling club. This photograph was taken *c.*1890.

127. Mrs. William Blackwell (neé Mary Shelley), a member of Rochford Methodist church.

128. The most popular form of sport in Rochford in the mid-19th century was following on foot the Rochford Beagles. The pack belonged to Teddy Jackson, manager of the local bank, seen here at 86 years of age with his sister, Rachel, aged 84 years. The beagles were housed in kennels in Back Lane, Rochford, and at Hawkwell.

129. *Anne Boleyn Hotel, c.*1900.

130. The *Anne Boleyn* estate was a popular rendezvous for gypsies. In this picture, taken about 1900, they are lining up with their caravans outside the *Anne Boleyn* ready for the road.

131. *Horse and Groom Inn, c.1860.*

132. *Horse and Groom Inn, c.1870.*

133. *Three Ashes Inn*, Southend Road, Rochford (formerly Eastwood), *c*.1900.

134. *White Horse Inn*, *c*.1900.

135.   *Cock Inn*, Hall Road, *c*.1900.

136.   The old *Shepherd and Dog Inn*, Ballards Gore.

137. The old *Shepherd and Dog Inn* after restoration. It is now a beautiful private residence. The present *Shepherd and Dog*, opposite, is pink-washed and was formerly thatched. It was built about 1935 and has appeared in television serials.

COACH DRIVES

THE ANCHOR HOTEL

THRESHAM (CHURCH'END) NEAR ROCHFORD

SOUTH STREET, ROCHFORD

"THE ANCHOR", FAMBRIDGE FERRY.

FAMBRIDGE FERRY

CANEWDON CHURCH

VIA

ROCHFORD

138. So pretty is the countryside around Rochford that coach operators arranged tours to and from Southend seafront to Rochford and the nearby villages. Note the old stage coach (top right-hand corner) passing through South Street.

139. Stambridge Mill, *c.*1920.

140. Stambridge Mill. A collection of barges are loading up with corn for the London market, *c*.1918. In high summer the marshes are covered with an impressive purple carpet of sea lavender.

141. Stambridge Mill about 1920, with a corn barge awaiting high tide before setting off with its cargo for the London market.

142.   Rochford-on-Sea near Stambridge Mill, *c.*1920, a favourite venue for family outings.

143.   Palm Beach near Stambridge Mill showing the barge *Joy*, *c.*1935.

144. Stambridge Village Street, *c*.1890.

145. Stambridge Village Street, 1910.

146. Ashingdon Road at its junction with New Hall Gardens, *c*.1920.

147. Ashingdon village, *c*.1920. This horse and cart coming down Ashingdon Hill is passing (on the left) part of the Vale of Assandune where the Battle of Assandune was fought in 1016 between Edmund Ironside and the victorious King Canute.

148.   A recent view of the site of the Battle of Assandune, 1016.

149.   The *Anchor Hotel*, South Fambridge. Visitors setting out for a charabanc ride, *c*.1912.

150. Paglesham, noted for its oysters and its smugglers. The coach waits outside the *Punch Bowl Inn* where many a smuggler's plot was hatched. This photograph was taken *c*.1910.

151. Church Road, Barling, *c*.1910, showing the weir pond.

152. Cockethurst Farm, Eastwood, *c.*1900. The beautiful Elizabethan creeper-covered house was once the home of the Vassals whose forebear, John Vassal, had a part share in the ownership of the *Mayflower* which carried the Pilgrim Fathers to America.

153. An Eastwood lane between the wars, *c.*1920.

154. Church of St Lawrence and All Saints, Eastwood. Built in Norman times, its greatest treasure is the priest's room originally used by the monks who walked from Prittlewell Priory to minister at the services. It is now the Vicar's vestry.

155. Interior of the beautiful Norman church at Eastwood.

156. Foulness Island. Under Crown ownership, the only access to the island prior to the construction of the present road in 1920 was along the Broomway, across the sands at low tide. The path was marked by broomsticks sticking out of the sand. Many lives were lost through drowning especially in fog. Foulness is internationally renowned as a haven for Brent Geese, and is their recognised breeding ground.

157. Girls' Training Corps (No. 650 Company), 1942. This photograph was taken in the grounds of 'Cottawight', Great Wakering. These cadets from Rochford and Wakering were undergoing pre-service training prior to entering H.M. Forces. The author, as officer-commanding, is seated in the centre.

158.   Opening of Rochford British Restaurant, 1942. Local councils set up British restaurants during World War Two to help the public eke out their meagre rations. Rochford's was situated in South Street. This picture shows Lord Woolton, Minister of Food, about to enter the restaurant with Harold Rankin, the Council's chairman, and S. C. Harris, the Council Clerk.

159.   Lord Woolton congratulates the Council on its successful venture and formally declares the Rochford British Restaurant open.

160. & 161.   East coast floods, 1953. The area was hard hit by floods which breached the sea walls in several places. Twelve people were drowned. The photograph above shows members of the Council's staff sorting food received from Australia, in the Council Chamber at Rochford prior to distribution. The photograph below shows the distribution of food to flood victims.

Bibliography

Benton, P., *History of Rochford Hundred*, 1880 *et seq.*
Blount, *Fragmenta Antiquitatis*, 1679
Burrows, J. W., *Southend-on-Sea and District*, 1909
Camden, *Survey of the British Isles*, 1522, 1610, 1637
Court Rolls
Glennie, D., *Our Town*, 1959
Holinshed, *History of Essex*
Hone, *Every Day Book*, 1827
Jacob, *Law Dictionary*, 1724
Kenny, *Laws of England*, 1889
London Standard, 1877
Morant P., *The History and Antiquities of the County of Essex*, 1768
Noble, *Historical and Geographical Survey of Rochford Hundred*, 1867
Pevsner, N., *Buildings of England*, 1953
Pollitt, W., *Archaeology of Rochford Hundred and South-East Essex*
Royal Commission on Historical Monuments, vol. IV, London, 1923
Salmon, *History of Essex*, 1740
Southend Standard
Weever, *Funeral Monuments*, 1631
Winstanley, *The New Help to Discourse*, 1669
Wright, *History of Essex*, 1835

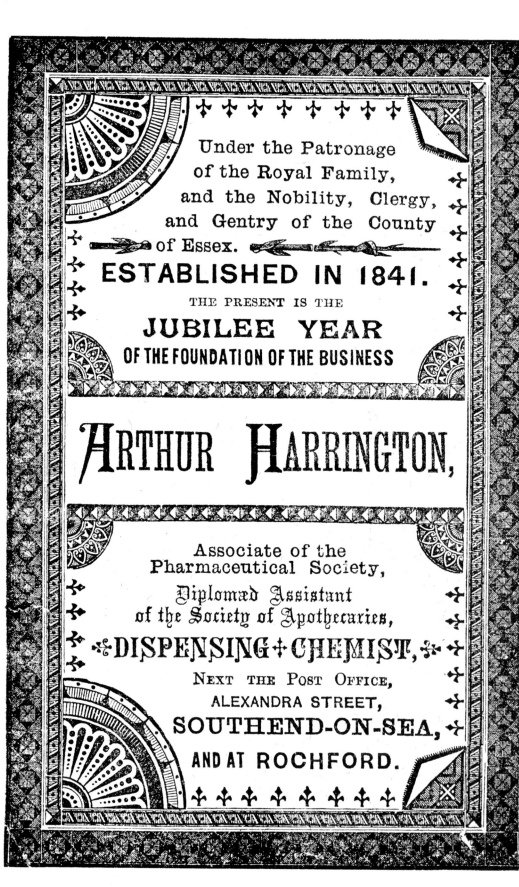